URINETOWN
THE MUSICAL

Photos by Joan Marcus

ISBN 0-634-07017-7

HAL•LEONARD®
CORPORATION
7777 W. BLUEMOUND RD. P.O. BOX 13819 MILWAUKEE, WI 53213

In Australia Contact:
Hal Leonard Australia Pty. Ltd.
22 Taunton Drive P.O. Box 5130
Cheltenham East, 3192 Victoria, Australia
Email: ausadmin@halleonard.com

Visit Hal Leonard Online at
www.halleonard.com

Jennifer Laura Thompson, Hunter Foster

CONTENTS

Nancy Opel

Jeff McCarthy, Spencer Kayden

(left to right) Lawrence E. Street, Victor W. Hawks, John Cullum, Rachel Coloff, Megan Lawrence

Jeff McCarthy and cast

URINETOWN

Music and Lyrics by MARK HOLLMANN
Book and Lyrics by GREG KOTIS

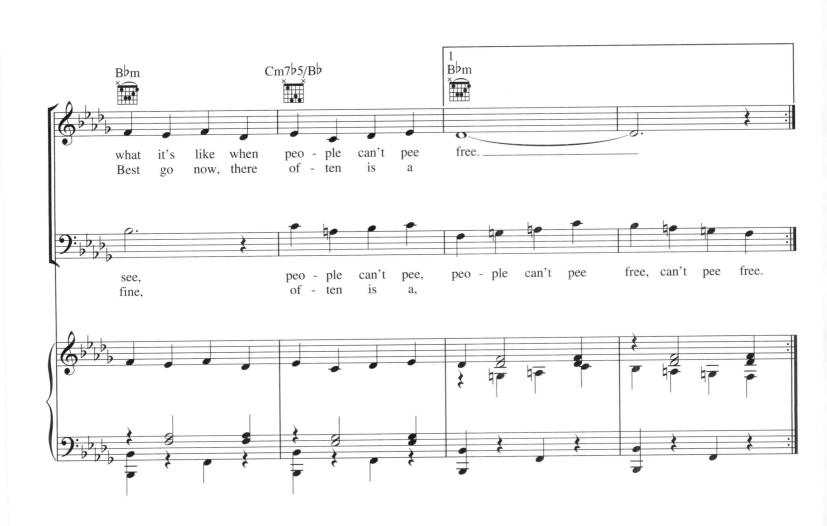

IT'S A PRIVILEGE TO PEE

Music and Lyrics by MARK HOLLMANN
Book and Lyrics by GREG KOTIS

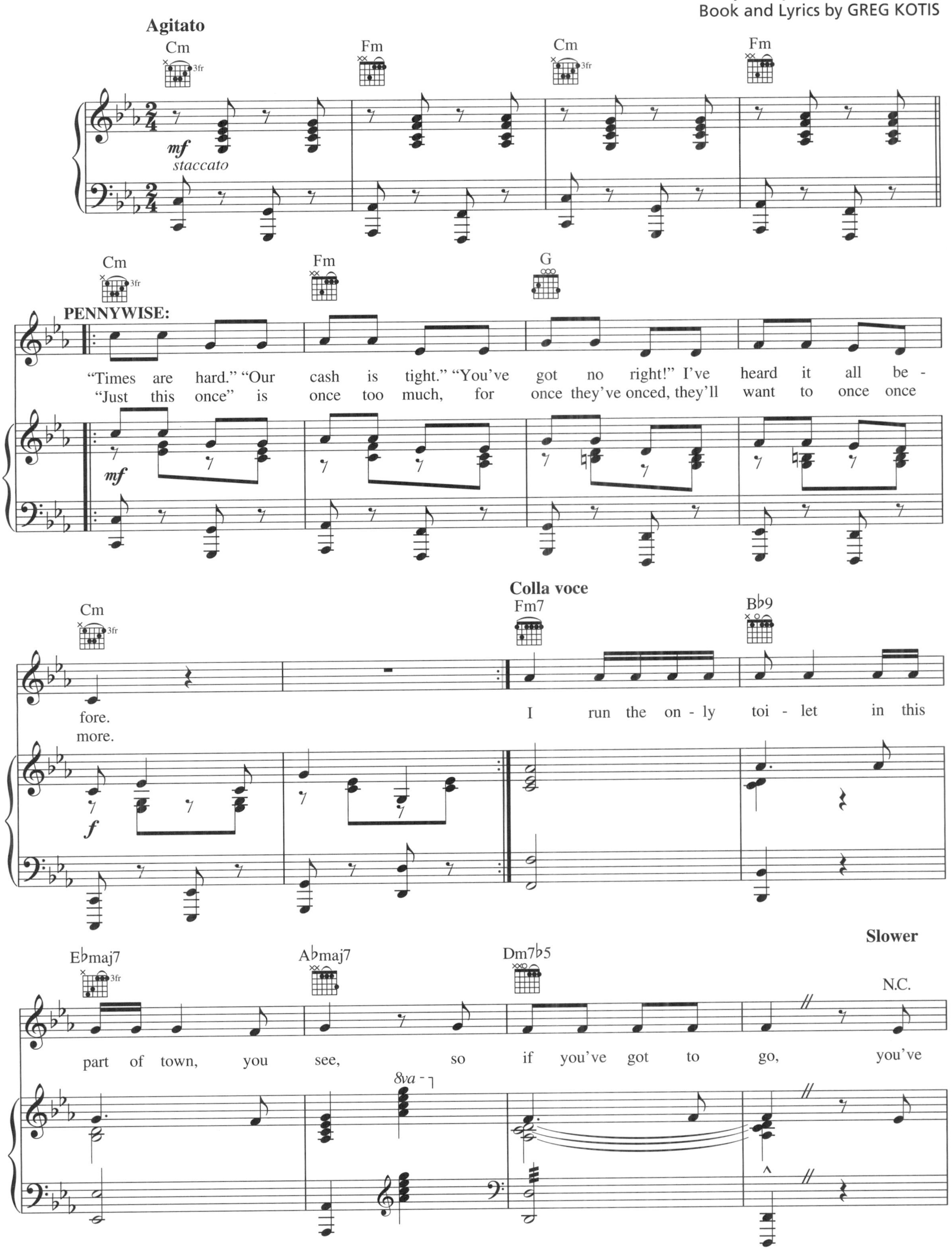

Agitato
Cm
Fm
Cm
Fm
mf
staccato
Cm
Fm
G
PENNYWISE:
"Times are hard." "Our cash is tight." "You've got no right!" I've heard it all be -
"Just this once" is once too much, for once they've onced, they'll want to once once
mf
Cm
Colla voce
Fm7
Bb9
fore.
more.
I run the on - ly toi - let in this
f
Eb maj7
Ab maj7
Dm7b5
Slower
N.C.
part of town, you see, so if you've got to go, you've
8va

19

MISTER CLADWELL

Music and Lyrics by MARK HOLLMANN
Book and Lyrics by GREG KOTIS

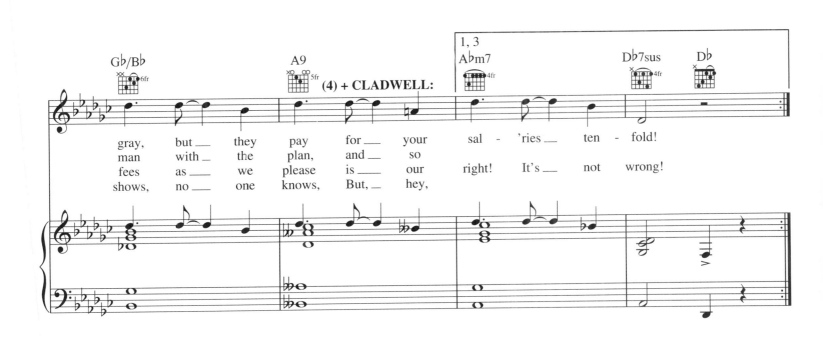

FOLLOW YOUR HEART

Music and Lyrics by MARK HOLLMANN
Book and Lyrics by GREG KOTIS

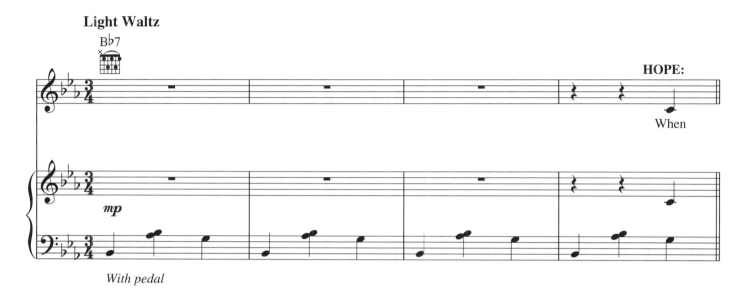

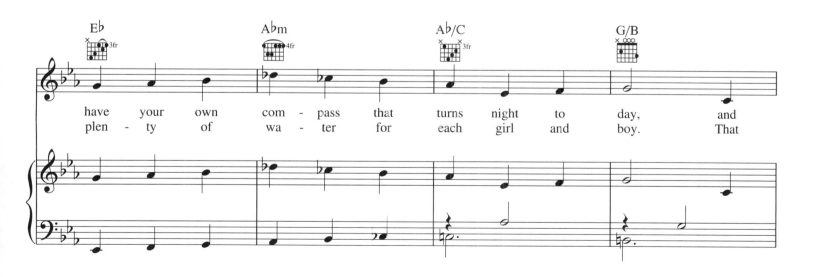

waiting to start. No anger or badness, just

Slower

laughter and gladness, if only I follow your

Slowly, in tempo

heart.

LOOK AT THE SKY

Words and Music by MARK HOLLMANN
Book and Lyrics by GREG KOTIS

DON'T BE THE BUNNY

Music and Lyrics by MARK HOLLMANN
Book and Lyrics by GREG KOTIS

Briskly, with a swagger

ACT ONE FINALE

Music and Lyrics by MARK HOLLMANN
Book and Lyrics by GREG KOTIS

Furious March tempo

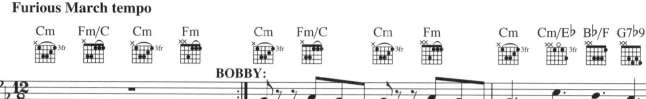

BOBBY:

Free! Peo-ple are free! How can a fee en-slave us?

See how we can be, free from the chains he gave us! We're suf-fer-ing now such

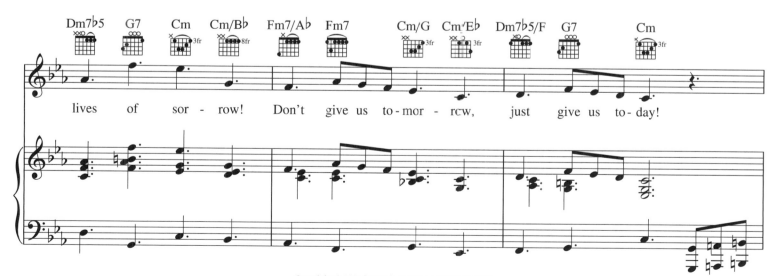

lives of sor-row! Don't give us to-mor-row, just give us to-day!

62

* Men sing one octave lower, Pennywise as written.

WHAT IS URINETOWN?

Music and Lyrics by MARK HOLLMANN
Book and Lyrics by GREG KOTIS

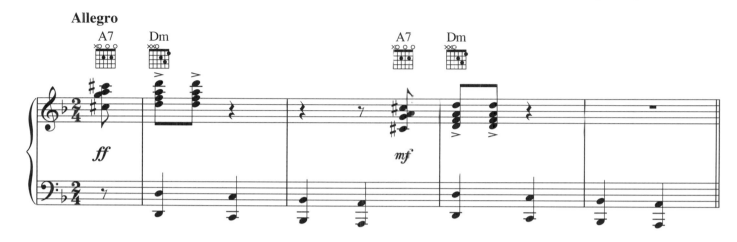

(1) LITTLE BECKY
(2) CLADWELL
(3) BOBBY

What is U - rine - town? U - rine - town's the end!
What is U - rine - town? U - rine - town's a tool! An
What is U - rine - town? U - rine - town's a lie! A

(1) HOT BLADES HARRY

Swift and bru - tal pun - ish - ment, no need now to pre - tend! The
in - stru - ment of pow - er to en - force my i - ron rule! So
means to keep the poor in check un - til the day they die! I

Dm   A7   Dm

trap - door's sprung and   then you're hung, and   when they cut you down,   they'll
send your troops to   all the stoops and   let them un - der - stand,   if
did not shirk their   dirt - y work, but   things are dif - f'rent now!   We'll

(1) THE POOR
(2) ALL
(3) BOBBY &
     JOSEPHINE

Gm   Dm   A7   Dm

box you up and   ship you out and   call it U - rine - town!   They'll
Hope is not re -   turned, it's U - rine - town for   all the land!   If
fight for right with   all our might un - til   we win some - how!   We'll

f

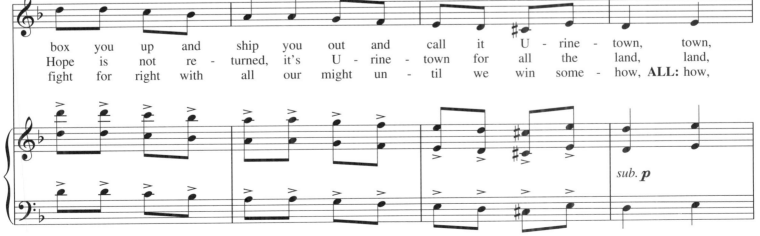

N.C.

box you up and   ship you out and   call it U - rine - town,   town,
Hope is not re -   turned, it's U - rine - town for   all the land,   land,
fight for right with   all our might un - til   we win some - how, **ALL:** how,

sub. p

town,   town,   town! _____
land,   land,   land! _____
how,   how,   how! _____

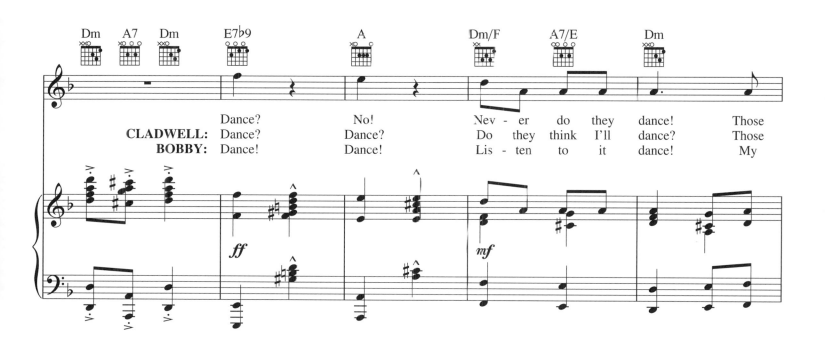

CLADWELL: Dance?   No!   Nev - er do they dance! Those
CLADWELL: Dance?   Dance?   Do they think I'll dance? Those
BOBBY: Dance!   Dance!   Lis - ten to it dance! My

peo - ple down in U - rine - town, they nev - er get the chance!
peo - ple with my daugh - ter want to make me change my stance!
heart is like a stal - lion rac - ing through a great ex - panse!

Danc - ing, for - get it! Nev - er, na - da, nope! Un -
Stance, dance, for - get it! Nev - er, na - da, nein! I'll
Can - yons of free - dom, that's where it will waltz, per -

less it's at the bot - tom of a rope!
teach them not to take from me what's mine!
form - ing cor - o - nar - y som - er -

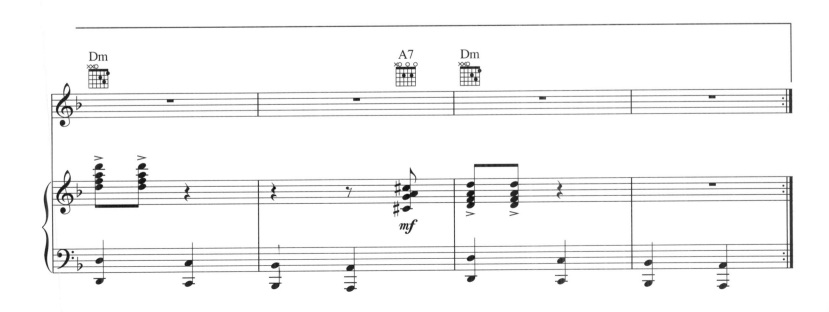

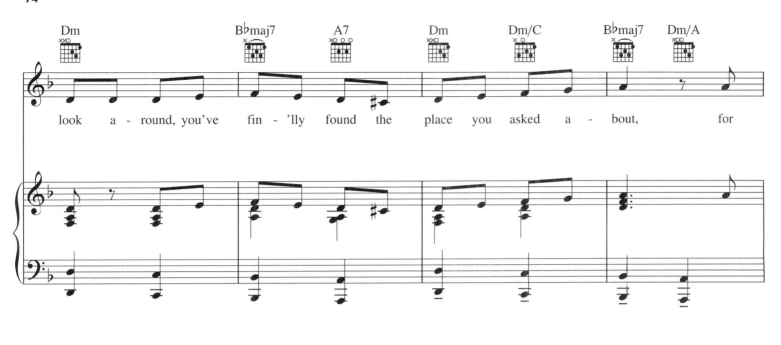

RUN, FREEDOM, RUN!

Music and Lyrics by MARK HOLLMANN
Book and Lyrics by GREG KOTIS

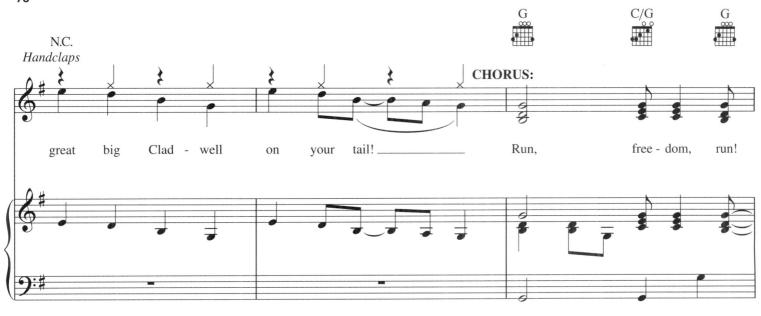

great big Clad - well on your tail! _____ Run, free - dom, run!

And he's put his hench - men on your trail! _____

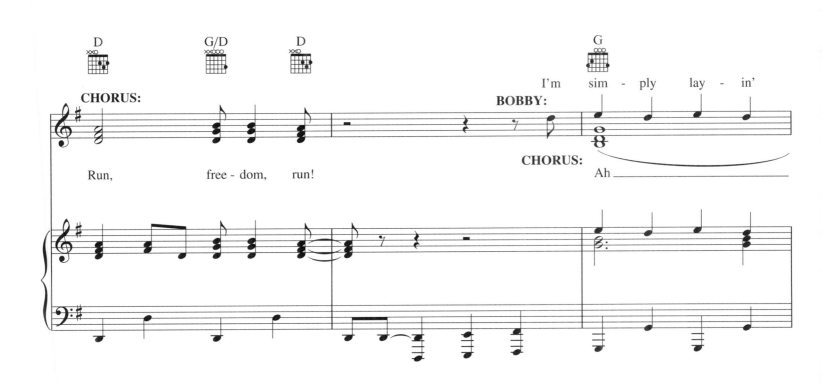

Run, free - dom, run!

I'm sim - ply lay - in'

Ah _____

WHY DID I LISTEN TO THAT MAN?

Music and Lyrics by MARK HOLLMANN
Book and Lyrics by GREG KOTIS

TELL HER I LOVE HER

Music and Lyrics by MARK HOLLMANN
Book and Lyrics by GREG KOTIS

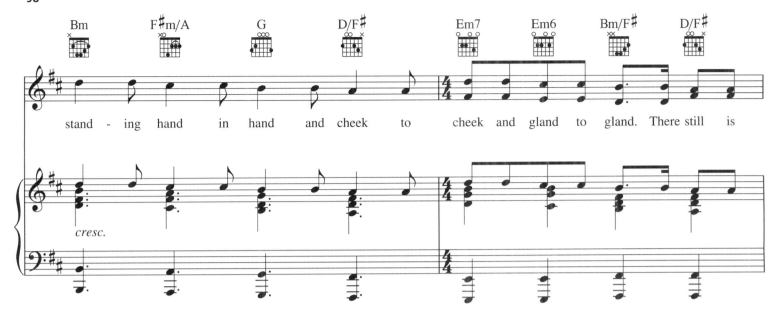

stand - ing hand in hand and cheek to cheek and gland to gland. There still is

cresc.

Slower

hope, I see it, in this land.

LITTLE SALLY:

JOSEPHINE: *Yes?*

BOBBY &
LITTLE SALLY:

If on - ly...

If on - ly...

f

poco rit.

mp

OTHERS: *Yes?!!*
LITTLE SALLY: *And then... he expired.*

A tempo

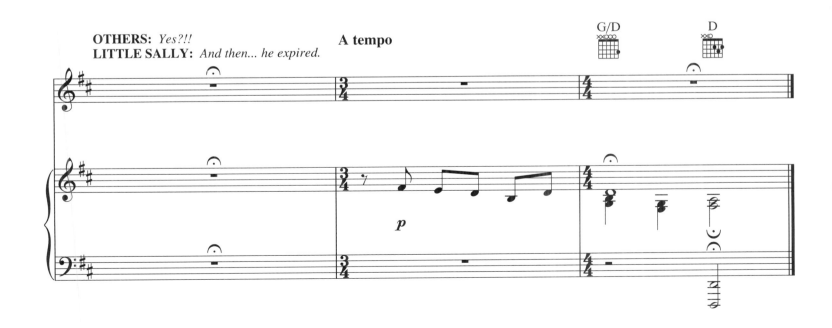

p

WE'RE NOT SORRY

Music and Lyrics by MARK HOLLMANN
Book and Lyrics by GREG KOTIS

F   F/A   C7/G   C7   Dm/A   Ddim/A   A7   Dm/A   Bb/G#   A7   Dm

Stra - di - va - ri:___ He's not sor - ry!___ Not a ___ shred!

N.C.

THE POOR:

He's not sor - ry! ___ He's not

Bb7

sor - ry! ___ He's not sor - ry! ___

Ebm   Ebm/Gb   Bb7/F   Bb7   Gb   Gb/Bb   Db7/Ab   Db7

JOSEPHINE:

You ___ who fly the ___ blimp ___ of e - vil ___

Lyrics:
shun __ up-heav-al __ in the __ air!

SOUPY SUE:
Then __ ask why the __ ride __ gets jar-ry! __

JOSEPHINE & LITTLE SALLY:
Now you're sor-ry __ you're up __ there!

THE POOR:
Now you're sor-ry! __ Now you're

102

WE'RE NOT SORRY - REPRISE

Music and Lyrics by MARK HOLLMANN
Book and Lyrics by GREG KOTIS

I SEE A RIVER

Music and Lyrics by MARK HOLLMANN
Book and Lyrics by GREG KOTIS

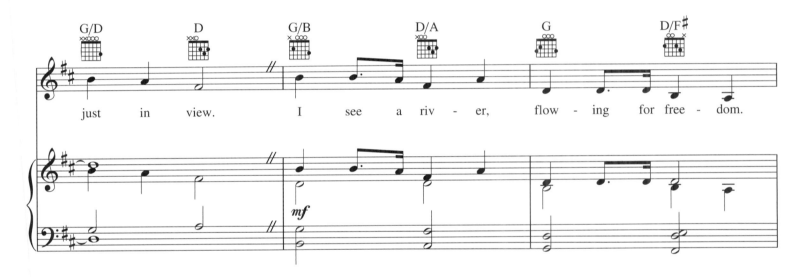

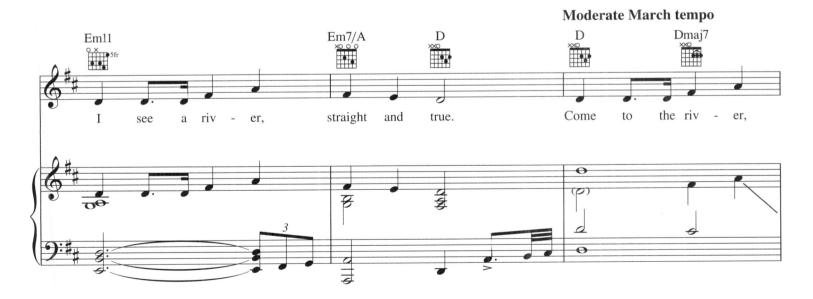

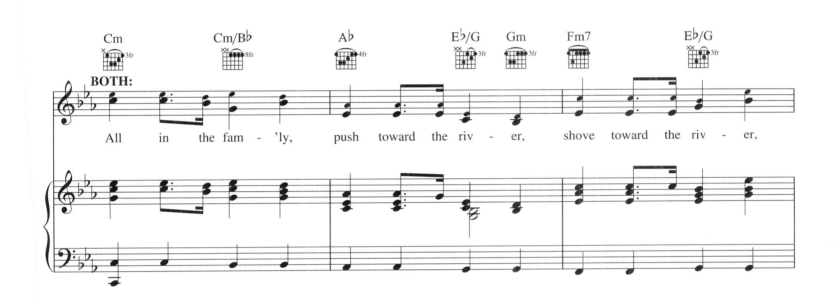